Favc

Cake Mix

Recipes

100 Quick & Easy
Recipes

SOUTHERN SOUP JOCKEYS

Graphics by Cheryl Seslar

ISBN-13: 978-1517611842

Contents

Cake Mix Recipes

All of us who love to bake enjoy putting on an apron, getting out the flour, sugar, eggs and make a downright old-fashioned mess of the kitchen. We all have a few family recipes that are go-to favorites. You may have Grandma Jean's red velvet cake recipe or perhaps Aunt Goldie's best-lemon-squares-on-earth recipe that you lovingly make for special occasions or family requests.

However, with the busy lives and schedules we all have, sometimes you just need to whip up a tasty dessert with no fuss or muss. This collection fills that niche in your repertoire of need-it-now recipes.

Keep a couple boxes of ready-to-use cake mixes on your pantry shelf. With the addition of just a few simple ingredients, you'll have a cake, cookie, bar, quick bread or coffee cake ready in the time it takes to heat up the oven. Last minute desserts are a breeze and clean-up is a snap. You'll always be ready for unexpected guests or impromptu potluck suppers, and what's even better; no one will know you haven't spent hours on one of the best desserts they've had in years!

BREAD

Breads

Pistachio Bread

Bread:

1 (16.5 oz.) package yellow cake mix
5 tablespoons + 1 teaspoon flour
1 (3.4 oz.) package pistachio instant pudding
4 eggs
1 cup sour cream
1/4 cup vegetable oil
1/2 cup nuts, chopped
3/4 cup maraschino cherries

Cinnamon-sugar mixture:

1/2 cup sugar
2 teaspoons cinnamon

Preheat oven to 350 degrees F. Spray 2 9x5x3-inch loaf pans with non-stick cooking spray. In a small bowl, mix sugar and cinnamon together; dust the loaf pans with 1/3 of the cinnamon-sugar mixture.

In a large bowl, mix all bread ingredients together and pour into prepared pans. Sprinkle tops with remainder of cinnamon-sugar mixture. Bake at 350 degrees F for 45 to 60 minutes. Cool on wire rack.

Lemon Poppy Seed Bread

1 (16.5 oz.) package yellow or lemon cake mix
5 tablespoons + 1 teaspoon flour
1 cup boiling water
1 (3.4 oz.) package instant lemon pudding
4 eggs
1/4 cup poppy seeds
1/4 cup vegetable oil

Preheat oven to 350 degrees F. In a large bowl, mix all ingredients above together for 3 minutes. Spray 2 8x4x2-inch loaf pans with non-stick cooking spray. Pour batter into loaf pans. Bake at 350 degrees F for 50 to 60 minutes. While still hot, run a knife around the edge of the loaf pan and top with glaze.

Glaze:

3/4 cup sugar
1/4 cup lemon juice
1/2 teaspoon almond extract
2 teaspoons melted butter
Combine all glaze ingredients and pour over hot bread.

Citrus Streusel Quick Bread

1 (16.5 oz.) package lemon or orange cake mix, divided
5 tablespoons flour
2 tablespoons brown sugar, packed
1 teaspoon cinnamon
1 tablespoon cold margarine or butter
1/2 cup pecans or black walnuts, chopped
1 (3.4 oz.) package instant vanilla pudding
4 eggs
1 cup sour cream
1/3 cup vegetable oil

Glaze:

1 cup confectioners' sugar
2 to 3 tablespoons milk

Preheat oven to 350 degrees F. In a small bowl, combine 2 tablespoons of cake mixture, brown sugar and cinnamon; cut in cold margarine or butter until crumbly. Stir in pecans or black walnuts; set aside.

In a large bowl, combine cake mix and flour. Add pudding, eggs, sour cream and oil. With an electric mixer, beat for 2 minutes on medium speed. Pour into 2 greased and floured 8x4x2-inch loaf pans; sprinkle with nut mixture. Bake at 350 degrees F for 45 to 50 minutes, or until a toothpick inserted near center comes out clean. Cool in pans for 10 minutes before removing to a wire rack.

Glaze: Combine confectioners' sugar and milk. Drizzle on warm bread.

Strawberry Banana Bread

1 (16.5 oz.) package strawberry cake mix
3 medium bananas
1/3 cup vegetable oil
3 eggs

Preheat oven to 350 degrees F. In a large bowl, mash bananas. Add cake mix, oil and eggs; blend well for 2 minutes. Spray a 9x5x3-inch loaf pan with non-stick cooking spray. Pour batter into loaf pan. Bake at 350 degrees F for 40 to 45 minutes or until passes the toothpick test.

Variation: For banana bread, substitute a white, yellow or butter pecan cake mix and optionally add 1 cup of chopped nuts.

Pumpkin Bread

1 (16.5 oz.) package spice cake mix
5 tablespoons + 1 teaspoon flour
3/4 cup granulated sugar
1 (15 oz.) can of solid-pack pumpkin
1/4 cup milk
2 eggs, beaten
1 teaspoon pumpkin pie spice

Preheat oven to 350 degrees F. Spray 2 8x4x2-inch loaf pans with non-stick cooking spray. In a large bowl, combine cake mix and sugar. Add pumpkin, milk and eggs; beat well for 2 minutes or until smooth. Add optional ingredients, if desired. Pour batter into loaf pans. Bake at 350 degrees F for 55 to 60 minutes or until passes the toothpick test.

Optional ingredients: 1/3 cup raisins, 1/3 cup walnut pieces, 1/2 cup chocolate chips or mini chocolate chips.

COOKIES

Cookies
German Chocolate Cookies

Topping:

1 cup sugar
1 cup evaporated milk
1/2 cup margarine, softened
3 egg yolks, beaten
1 teaspoon vanilla
1 1/2 cups flaked coconut
1 1/2 cups pecans, chopped

Cookies:
1 (16.5 oz.) package German chocolate cake mix
5 tablespoons + 1 teaspoon flour
1/3 cup margarine, melted

In a saucepan, combine sugar, evaporated milk, margarine, egg yolks and vanilla; mix well. Cook over medium heat for 10 to 12 minutes or until bubbly and thick, stirring frequently. Stir in coconut and pecans. Remove from heat. Cool to room temperature. Reserve 1 1/4 cups of topping; set aside.

Preheat oven to 350 degrees F. In a large bowl, combine cookie ingredients: cake mix, flour, margarine and remaining topping; stir until well combined. Shape dough into 1" balls. Place 2" apart on ungreased cookie sheet. Make a thumbprint indentation in center of ball. Fill each with rounded 1/2 teaspoon reserved topping mixture. Bake at 350 degrees F for 10 to 13 minutes or until set. Cool 5 minutes, remove from cookie sheets. Yield: 5 dozen cookies.

Cherry Topped Chocolate Cookies

1 (10 oz.) jar maraschino cherry halves
1 (16.5 oz.) package devil's food cake mix
5 tablespoons + 1 teaspoon flour
1/2 cup sour cream
1 egg
2 tablespoons confectioner's sugar

Preheat oven to 375 degrees F. Drain cherries; place on paper towel and pat dry. In a large bowl, beat cake mix, flour, sour cream, and egg with an electric mixer at medium speed until light in color (batter will be stiff). Use greased hands to shape dough into 1-inch balls; place 2 inches apart on greased baking sheet.

Press 1 cherry half into center of each cookie. Bake at 375 degrees F for 8 to 10 minutes. Cool cookies on baking sheet for 2 minutes, transfer to a wire rack to cool. Sprinkle cookies with confectioners' sugar.

Yield: 4 dozen cookies.

Pina Colada Cookies

1/4 cup butter, softened
1 (8 oz.) package cream cheese, softened
1 egg yolk
1/2 teaspoon rum extract
1/2 cup pineapple juice
1 (16.5 oz.) package yellow cake mix
5 tablespoons + 1 teaspoon flour
1/2 cup flaked coconut
Yellow sugar, for decoration

Preheat oven to 375 degrees F. In a large bowl, cream together butter and cream cheese. Blend in the egg yolk, rum extract and pineapple juice. Combine cake mix and flour; add the cake mixture, one-third at a time, mixing well after each addition. Add the coconut and blend well. Cover the mixture; refrigerate for 30 minutes.

Drop the dough by teaspoonful onto an ungreased baking sheet. Sprinkle cookies with yellow sugar. Bake at 375 degrees F for 11 minutes or until light brown. Cool slightly before removing from baking sheet.

Yield: 4 to 5 dozen cookies.

Peanut Butter Cookies

1 (16.5 oz.) package yellow or chocolate cake mix
5 tablespoons + 1 teaspoon flour
1 cup peanut butter
2 eggs
1/2 cup vegetable oil or canola oil
2 tablespoons water

Preheat oven to 350 degrees F. In a large bowl, combine oil, water, eggs and peanut butter. Add dry cake mix and flour; blend well. Drop by teaspoonful on an ungreased cookie sheet. Flatten cookies slightly with a fork. Bake at 350 degrees F for 10 to 12 minutes. Cool on cookie sheet for 1 minute; remove to a rack to cool.

Yield: 4 to 5 dozen cookies.

Double Chocolate Nuggets

1 (16.5 oz.) package devil's food cake mix
5 tablespoons + 1 teaspoon flour
1/2 cup vegetable oil or canola oil
2 eggs
1 (6 oz.) package chocolate chips
1 teaspoon peppermint extract
1 cup nuts, chopped

Preheat oven to 350 degrees F. In a large bowl, combine cake mix, flour, oil and eggs. Stir in chocolate chips, peppermint extract and nuts. Drop by teaspoonful onto ungreased cookie sheet. Bake at 350 degrees F for 10 to 12 minutes, until cookie tests done with a toothpick.

Yield: 3 to 4 dozen cookies.

Lollipop Cookies

1 package rainbow chip or confetti cake mix
5 tablespoons + 1 teaspoon flour
2 eggs
3/4 cup water
24 popsicle sticks
1 carton frosting

Preheat oven to 375 degrees F. In a large bowl, beat cake mix, flour, eggs and water with electric mixer on low speed for 30 seconds. Beat on high speed for an additional 2 minutes. On ungreased baking sheets, drop dough by rounded tablespoons 3 inches apart. Insert a popsicle stick 1 1/2-inches into the dough.

Bake at 375 degrees F for 8 to 11 minutes or until cookie touched lightly in the center feels springy and the indentation fills up when removing finger. Cool on baking sheet for 1 minute; transfer to wire racks. Frost and decorate.

Yield: 20 to 24 cookies.

Cherry Chip Cookies

1 (16.5 oz.) package cherry chip cake mix
1/4 cup flour
1/2 cup vegetable oil
1 egg
1/4 cup water

Preheat oven to 350 degrees F. In a large bowl, combine cake mix, flour, oil, egg and water. Drop by teaspoonful on ungreased cookie sheet. Bake at 350 degrees F for 10 to 12 minutes.

Yield: 2 to 3 dozen cookies.

Other Goodies

Cinnamon Rolls

1 box yellow or white cake mix
5 1/2 cups flour
3 (1/4 oz. each) pkgs. yeast
2 1/2 cups warm water

Filling:

1/2 cup butter or margarine, melted
1 cup sugar
3 teaspoons cinnamon

In a large bowl, combine water and yeast; set aside. In another large bowl, mix cake mix and flour together. Add yeast mixture and mix well by hand. Place in a greased bowl; turn once and cover. Let rise until doubled in size.

Roll out to approximately 8x30". Brush melted margarine on dough. Mix sugar and cinnamon together. Sprinkle over dough. Roll up and cut in approximately thirty 1" pieces. Place in greased pan. Let rise until double in size. Bake in preheated oven at 350 degrees F for 20 to 25 minutes. Frost while warm.

Variation: May add nuts and raisins.

Yield: 30 cinnamon rolls.

Blueberry Cobbler

2 packages white cake mix
1/2 cup water
6 cups blueberries
1 1/2 cups sugar
1/8 teaspoon salt
1 (8 oz.) carton refrigerated whipped topping

Preheat oven to 350 degrees F. Spray a 13x9x2-inch baking dish with non-stick cooking spray. In a large bowl, mix one package of cake mix with 1/4 cup of water. Pour in prepared baking dish. Add blueberries to dish, then sugar and salt. In a large bowl, mix second package of cake mix with 1/4 cup of water. Pour over all in baking dish. Bake at 350 degrees F for 1 hour. Serve topped with whipped topping.

Cupcake Cones

24 flat-bottom ice cream cones, 2" to 3" high
1 package any flavor plain cake mix
2 cans prepared frosting
Plain or peanut chocolate candies
Candy sprinkles, toasted coconut or nuts, as desired

Preheat oven to 350 degrees F. Prepare cake mix according to package directions. Fill each cone with 3 tablespoons of batter. Place on ungreased cookie sheet about 3 inches apart, or place cones in muffin pans. Bake at 350 degrees F for 30 to 35 minutes, or until wooden pick inserted in the center comes out clean. Cool thoroughly. Frost and decorate with candies and nuts.

Yield: 24 cupcake cones.

Lemon Poppy Seed Muffins

1 (16.5 oz.) package lemon cake mix
3/4 cup flour
2/3 cup water
1/3 cup vegetable oil
2 eggs
1 tablespoon poppy seed

Preheat oven to 375 degrees F. Stir all ingredients together in a large bowl about 75 strokes. Fill muffin cups 1/2 full. Bake at 375 degrees F for 25 to 30 minutes.

Yield: 24 muffins.

Holiday Pancakes

2 cups packaged pound cake mix
1 1/3 cups milk
2 eggs
6 tablespoons butter, melted

In a large bowl, combine cake mix, milk, eggs and butter; mix well. Spoon batter on lightly greased griddle. Cook until top is bubbled and edges look done. Turn. Roll up jellyroll style. Top with whipped topping, fresh fruit, orange syrup, confectioners' sugar, etc.

Blueberry Muffins

1 package white cake mix
5 tablespoons + 1 teaspoon flour
3 eggs (large)
2/3 cup milk
1/3 cup vegetable oil
2 teaspoons baking powder
2 cups frozen blueberries (do not thaw)

Preheat oven to 375 degrees F. In a large bowl, combine cake mix, flour, eggs, milk, oil, and baking powder. Mix 2 minutes on high with electric mixer. Fold in frozen blueberries. Fill paper-lined muffin cups 3/4 full. Bake for 15 to 22 minutes at 375 degrees F.

Yield: 24 muffins.

Filled Cupcakes

1 package chocolate cake mix
1 (8 oz.) cream cheese, softened
1/3 cup sugar
1 egg
1/8 teaspoon salt
1 (6 oz.) package semi-sweet chocolate chips

Mix cake mix according to package. Fill cups in muffin pan two-thirds full. In a separate bowl, combine cream cheese with sugar. Beat in egg and salt. Stir in chocolate chips. Drop one rounded teaspoon of mixture on each cupcake. Follow cake mix directions for baking time and temperature.

Yield: 24 cupcakes.

Bundt Cakes

Pineapple Pudding Cake

1 (16.5 oz.) package yellow cake mix
5 tablespoons + 1 teaspoon flour
1 (3.4 oz.) package pistachio instant pudding
1 (8 1/4 oz.) can crushed pineapple (undrained)
4 eggs
1 cup sour cream
1/4 cup vegetable oil

Preheat oven to 350 degrees F. Combine all ingredients in a large bowl. With electric mixer, beat at medium speed for 2 minutes.

Grease and flour a Bundt pan. Pour batter into pan. Bake at 350 degrees F for 50 to 55 minutes. Cool in pan for 15 minutes.

Butterscotch-Chocolate Bundt Cake

1 (16.5 oz.) package yellow cake mix
5 tablespoons + 1 teaspoon flour
4 eggs
1 cup water
1 (3.4 oz.) instant butterscotch pudding mix
1/2 cup vegetable oil
1/2 cup chocolate syrup

Preheat oven to 350 degrees F. In a large bowl, combine cake mix, flour, eggs, water, pudding mix and oil; beat 4 minutes at medium speed. Pour 2/3 of the batter in a greased and floured Bundt pan.

Mix remaining batter with chocolate syrup. Pour over batter in pan. Bake at 350 degrees F for 1 hour or until done. Cool upright in pan for 30 minutes. Invert plate and cool. Sprinkle with confectioners' sugar.

Kahlua Cake

Cake:

1 (16.5 oz.) package yellow cake mix
5 tablespoons + 1 teaspoon flour
4 eggs
1 cup vegetable oil
1/4 cup sugar
1 (5.9 oz.) package instant chocolate pudding
2/3 cup water
1/4 cup vodka
1/4 cup Kahlua

Glaze:

1/2 cup confectioners' sugar
1/4 cup Kahlua

Preheat oven to 350 degrees F. Combine all cake ingredients in a large bowl. Pour into a greased and floured Bundt pan. Bake at 350 degrees F for 50 to 60 minutes or until cake springs back when lightly touched. Cool 10 minutes. Turn pan over on plate. In a small bowl, mix glaze ingredients together. Poke holes in cake with fork and pour glaze over cake.

Chocolate Bundt Cake

Flour (for dusting pan)
1 (16.5 oz.) package devil's food or dark chocolate fudge cake mix
5 tablespoons + 1 teaspoon flour
1 (3.95 oz.) package chocolate instant pudding mix
4 large eggs
1 cup dairy sour cream
1/2 cup warm water
1/2 cup vegetable oil
1 1/2 cups semi-sweet chocolate chips

Preheat oven to 350 degrees F. Lightly spray a 12-cup Bundt pan with non-stick cooking spray; dust with flour. In a large bowl, combine cake mix, flour, pudding mix, eggs, sour cream, warm water and oil. Blend with electric mixer on low speed for 1 minute. On medium speed, beat for 2 to 3 minutes more. Fold in chocolate chips, stirring well.

Pour batter into prepared pan; smooth with a rubber spatula. Bake at 350 degrees F for 45 to 50 minutes or until cake springs back when lightly touched and just starts to pull away from sides of pan. Remove from oven and place on a wire rack to cool. Run a knife around edge of cake and invert onto a serving platter.

Yield: 16 servings.

Spiced Tea Cake

Cake:

1 (16.5 oz.) package yellow cake mix
5 tablespoons + 1 teaspoon flour
1/2 cup sugar
1 tablespoon instant tea
1 teaspoon lemon juice
1 teaspoon cinnamon
1/2 teaspoon cloves
1 cup orange juice
3/4 cup vegetable oil
4 eggs

Preheat oven to 350 degrees F. Combine all cake ingredients in a large bowl. Beat for 2 minutes on medium speed. Pour mixture in a greased Bundt pan. Bake at 350 degrees F for 50 to 60 minutes. Cool 15 minutes.

Topping:

1 tablespoon margarine
2 tablespoons brown sugar, packed
2 tablespoons confectioners' sugar
1/4 cup nuts, chopped

Combine topping ingredients and drizzle over cake.

Coffee Cake

Batter:

1 (16.5 oz.) package yellow cake mix
5 tablespoons + 1 teaspoon flour
1 (3.4 oz.) box instant vanilla pudding
3/4 cup vegetable oil
3/4 cup water
4 eggs
1 teaspoon vanilla

Nut mixture:

1/2 cup nuts, chopped fine
1/4 cup white sugar
1 teaspoon cinnamon

Frosting:

1 cup confectioners' sugar
3 to 4 teaspoons milk
1/2 teaspoon vanilla
1/4 teaspoon almond flavoring

Preheat oven to 350 degrees F. Mix nut mixture ingredients and set aside. In a large bowl, combine cake mix, flour, pudding, oil and water; mix well. Add eggs and vanilla and beat 8 minutes.

Pour into greased Bundt cake pan: layer of batter, nut mixture layer, layer of batter, layer of nut mixture. Take knife and cut through batter. Bake at 350 degrees F for 40 to 45 minutes. Cool 8 to 10 minutes. Remove from pan. Combine frosting ingredients; frost cake.

Blackberry Cake

1 (16.5 oz.) package white cake mix
5 tablespoons + 1 teaspoon flour
1 (6 oz.) or 2 (3 oz.) packages blackberry gelatin
2/3 cup vegetable oil
2/3 cup blackberry juice
4 eggs

Preheat oven to 325 degrees F. Pour cake mix into a large bowl. Mix in flour. Add gelatin, blackberry juice, oil and eggs. Beat at medium speed for 2 minutes with electric mixer. Pour batter into a Bundt or small tube pan and bake at 325 degrees F for an hour and 15 minutes.

Golden Amaretto Cake

1 (16.5 oz.) package yellow cake mix
5 tablespoons + 1 teaspoon flour
1 package (5.9 oz.) instant vanilla pudding
3/4 cup Amaretto liqueur
1/4 teaspoon almond extract
1 cup confectioners' sugar
1/2 cup vegetable oil
4 eggs
1/2 cup confectioners' sugar
6 tablespoons Amaretto liqueur

Preheat oven to 350 degrees F. In a large bowl, combine cake mix, flour, vanilla pudding, 3/4 cup Amaretto liqueur, almond extract, confectioner's sugar, oil and eggs; mix well. Grease and lightly flour a 12 cup Bundt pan. Pour batter into pan. Bake at 350 degrees F for 45 to 50 minutes, or until cake springs back when lightly touched.

Combine 6 tablespoons Amaretto liqueur and confectioners' sugar. (Add a little water if needed.) Leaving cake in pan, poke holes in warm cake; pour Amaretto mixture over cake. Allow to cool in pan at least 2 hours.

Rum Cake

1/2 cup pecans, chopped
1 (16.5 oz.) package yellow cake mix
5 tablespoons + 1 teaspoon flour
4 eggs
1/2 cup cold water
1/2 cup vegetable oil
1/2 cup rum

Sauce:
1/2 cup margarine or butter
1 cup sugar
1/4 cup rum
1/4 cup water

Preheat oven to 325 degrees F. Spray a Bundt cake pan with non-stick cooking spray. Sprinkle pecans on bottom of Bundt pan. In a large bowl, combine cake mix, flour, eggs, water, oil and rum. Beat for 6 minutes on medium speed. Pour over nuts. Bake at 325 degrees F for 55 to 60 minutes, or until toothpick comes out clean.

Sauce: About 10 minutes before cake is done, bring sauce ingredients to a boil and cook 2 minutes, stirring constantly. When cake comes out of oven, carefully poke several holes in cake, loosen sides away from pan, and slowly pour sauce over cake in pan. Let sit until sauce is well absorbed, about 30 minutes. Invert onto plate. Yield: 12 to 16 servings.

Pistachio Nut Bundt Cake

1 (16.5 oz.) package white cake mix
5 tablespoons + 1 teaspoon flour
1 (3.4 oz.) package pistachio instant pudding
4 eggs
1/2 cup vegetable oil
1 cup water
3/4 cup chocolate syrup

Preheat oven to 350 degrees F. In a large bowl, combine cake mix, flour, pudding, eggs, oil and water. Beat according to directions on cake mix box. Pour 2/3 of batter into greased Bundt pan. Add Hershey syrup to rest of batter and pour over light batter. Bake at 350 degrees F for about 45 minutes. Cool for 10 minutes before removing from cake pan. Dribble thin chocolate icing over cake.

CAKES WITH FRUIT

Cakes With Fruit

Applesauce Spice Tube Cake

1 (16.5 oz.) package yellow cake mix
5 tablespoons + 1 teaspoon flour
1 cup applesauce
1 (3.4 oz.) package instant vanilla pudding
2 eggs
1/2 cup water
1/3 cup vegetable oil or canola oil
1 teaspoon cinnamon
1/4 teaspoon nutmeg
1/4 teaspoon cloves

Preheat oven to 350 degrees F. Combine all ingredients in a large bowl and beat at medium speed about 2 minutes. Pour into well-greased and floured 10 inch tube pan. Bake at 350 degrees F about 45 minutes. Cool 30 minutes in pan, then remove and let cool. Drizzle with icing, if desired.

Hawaiian Cake

1 package yellow cake mix
1 (20 oz.) can crushed pineapple

Topping:

1 (3.4 oz.) box instant vanilla pudding
1/2 cup milk
8 oz. refrigerated whipped topping
Coconut
Mandarin oranges
Nuts

Bake cake per box instructions using a 13x9x2-inch pan. While still hot, poke holes in cake and pour the crushed pineapple over the top. Cool. Stir together the pudding mix and milk, then mix with whipped topping. Spread over cake. Top with coconut, well-drained mandarin oranges and nuts, if desired. Cover and refrigerate 3 hours or overnight.

Pumpkin Crunch

1 (15 oz.) can pumpkin
1 (5 oz.) can evaporated milk
3/4 cup sugar
2 teaspoons pumpkin pie spice
2 eggs
1 package spice cake mix
3/4 cup margarine
1 cup nuts, chopped

Preheat oven to 350 degrees F. Mix pumpkin, evaporated milk, sugar, pumpkin pie spice and eggs. Pour into ungreased 13x9x2-inch baking dish. Sprinkle dry cake mix over top. Dot with margarine. Add nuts. Bake at 350 degrees F for 55 to 60 minutes. Serve with refrigerated whipped topping or ice cream.

Easy Cherry Cake Crisp

1 package yellow cake mix
1 (20 oz.) can crushed pineapple, undrained
1 (21 oz.) can cherry pie filling
1 cup pecans, chopped
1/2 cup butter or margarine

Preheat oven to 350 degrees F. Pour the undrained pineapple into a 13x9x2-inch pan, spreading evenly. Make a 2nd layer with the pie filling; spread evenly. Sprinkle dry cake mix on top of pie filling. Sprinkle nuts over cake mix. Place sliced butter or margarine pieces on top. Bake 48 to 52 minutes at 350 degrees F.

Pig Pickin' Cake

1 (16.5 oz.) package yellow cake mix
5 tablespoons + 1 teaspoon flour
1 (11 oz.) can mandarin oranges, with juice
1/2 cup vegetable oil
4 eggs

Preheat oven to 350 degrees F. In a large bowl, combine cake mix, flour, oranges with juice, oil and eggs. Pour into a 13x9x2-inch baking dish. Bake at 350 degrees F for 30 to 35 minutes or until done. Cool.

Topping:

1 (20 oz.) can crushed pineapple, drained
1 (3.4 oz.) box vanilla instant pudding
1 (16 oz.) carton refrigerated whipped topping

Mix dry pudding and pineapple together and then add whipped topping. Keep refrigerated.

Pineapple Upside-Down Cake

3 tablespoons butter or margarine
3/4 cup dark brown sugar, packed
Maraschino cherry halves
1 egg
1 (15 oz.) can sliced pineapple, drained (reserve juice)
1 (9 oz.) package one-layer yellow cake mix (if larger mix, use 2 cups of cake mix)

Place butter in a 9-inch round dish. Microwave on high about 45 seconds or until melted. Add brown sugar and mix well. Arrange pineapple slices over butter mixture, and place a maraschino cherry half in center of each pineapple slice.

Prepare cake mix according to instructions on package, using reserved pineapple juice in place of liquid. (Generally this is 1/2 cup juice, 1 egg and cake mix). Pour batter into dish and evenly distribute over surface. Microwave 6 to 8 minutes, turning dish twice during cooking time. Cake will spring back when lightly touched. Let stand 1 minute. Invert onto serving dish.

Punch Bowl Cake

1 package yellow cake mix
2 (3.4 oz. each) pkgs. vanilla instant pudding
2 (20 oz. each) cans crushed pineapple, drained
2 (21 oz. each) cans cherry pie filling
1 (16 oz.) container refrigerated whipped topping
Pecans
Maraschino cherries

Bake cake as directed on package. Break half of cake into small pieces and place in bottom of a punch bowl. Mix 1 package of pudding as directed on box and pour over cake. Drain 1 can of pineapple and pour over pudding. Next, put 1 can cherry pie filing, then half of whipped topping. Add nuts. Repeat layers and top with nuts and maraschino cherries.

Raspberry Shortcut Cake

2 cups mini marshmallows
1 (3 oz.) package raspberry jello
2 1/2 cups fresh raspberries
1 package yellow cake mix

Preheat oven to 350 degrees F. Grease bottom only of a 13x9x2" baking dish. Spread marshmallows over bottom of pan. Mix dry jello and raspberries together and set aside. Mix cake as directed on package and spread over marshmallows. Dribble jello mixture over batter. Bake at 350 degrees F for 40 to 45 minutes. Cool and serve with whipped topping.

Variation: Fresh chopped strawberries and strawberry jello may be used instead of raspberry.

Strawberry Cake

1 (16.5 oz.) package white cake mix
5 tablespoons + 1 teaspoon flour 1/4 cup flour
1 (3 oz.) package strawberry jello
1/2 cup water
4 eggs
5 oz. frozen strawberries or 1/2 cup of fresh berries
2/3 cup vegetable oil or canola oil

Preheat oven to 350 degrees F. Combine all ingredients in a large bowl and beat at medium speed for 4 minutes with mixer. Pour into an ungreased 13x9x2" baking dish. Bake at 350 degrees F for 30 minutes.

Frosting:

1/4 lb. margarine
1 (16 oz.) box confectioners' sugar

Combine margarine, confectioners' sugar and remaining strawberries. Mix with mixer until well blended. Frost cake when cooled.

Cherry-Nut Pound Cake

1 (16.5 oz.) package chocolate cake mix
5 tablespoons + 1 teaspoon flour
1 (3 oz.) box orange or pineapple jello (use dry)
4 eggs
2/3 cup cold water
2/3 cup vegetable oil
1/2 cup maraschino cherries, chopped
1/2 cup nuts, chopped

Preheat oven to 325 degrees F. In a large bowl, combine cake mix, flour, jello, eggs, water and oil. Beat at high speed for 5 minutes. Add cherries and nuts. Pour into a greased angel food cake pan. Bake at 325 degrees F in for 1 hour.

Pumpkin Pie Cake

1 package yellow cake mix
1 egg
1/4 cup margarine, melted
3 1/2 cups canned pumpkin
1/2 cup sugar
2/3 cup evaporated milk
2 teaspoons cinnamon
3 eggs

Topping:
1 cup cake mix
2 tablespoons margarine
3/4 cup sugar

Preheat oven to 350 degrees F. Reserve 1 cup cake mix for topping. Combine the remainder of cake mix, 1 egg and margarine in a medium bowl. Press mixture into 13x9x2" baking dish. In another bowl, combine pumpkin, sugar, milk, cinnamon and 3 eggs, mixing well. Pour gently over cake mix in baking dish. Add 2 tablespoons margarine and 3/4 cup sugar to reserved 1 cup of cake mix for topping. Sprinkle topping over pumpkin mixture. Bake at 350 degrees F for 55 minutes.

Apricot Dessert

1 (2 1/2 lb.) can apricots, cut up (reserve juice)
1 box butter brickle cake mix
1/2 cup melted butter
1 cup pecans

Preheat oven to 350 degrees F. Place cut up apricots and juice in bottom of 13x9x2" baking dish. Sprinkle cake mix over all; drizzle butter on top and add chopped nuts. Bake at 350 degrees F for 40 minutes or until browned.

Cherry Cheese Cake

1 package yellow cake mix
1/3 cup butter, softened
3 eggs
1 cup sugar
2 teaspoons vanilla
2 (8 oz.) pkgs. cream cheese, softened
2 cups sour cream
2 teaspoons vanilla (divided)
1 (21 oz.) can cherry pie filling

Preheat oven to 350 degrees F. With an electric mixer, beat cake mix, butter and 1 egg in large mixing bowl at low speed until crumbly. Press lightly in ungreased 13x9x2" baking pan. Beat 2 eggs, 3/4 cup sugar, 1 teaspoon vanilla and cream cheese until smooth and fluffy. Spread over cake mix mixture. Bake at 350 degrees F for 20 to 25 minutes or until set.

Mix sour cream, 1/4 cup sugar and 1 teaspoon vanilla. Spread over cheese mixture. Cool. Spread cherry pie filling over sour cream mixture. Cover and refrigerate at least 8 hours.

Yield: 16 to 18 servings.

Lemon Sheet Cake

1 (16.5 oz.) package lemon cake mix
5 tablespoons + 1 teaspoon flour
4 eggs
1 (15 3/4 oz.) can lemon pie filling

Preheat oven to 350 degrees F. In a large bowl, beat cake mix, flour and eggs until well mixed. Stir in pie filling. Spread into a greased 15x10x1" or 8x12x3" baking pan. Bake at 350 degrees F for 18 to 20 minutes or until passes the toothpick test. Cool on wire rack.

Frosting:

2 cups confectioners' sugar
1/2 cup butter or margarine, softened
1 (3 oz.) cream cheese, softened
1 1/2 teaspoons vanilla extract

In a small bowl, beat confectioners' sugar, butter or margarine and cream cheese until smooth. Stir in vanilla. Spread over cake. Refrigerate cake.

Yield: 30 to 35 servings.

Peaches and Cream Cake

1 (16.5 oz.) package yellow cake mix
5 tablespoons + 1 teaspoon flour
1 (3.4 oz.) box instant vanilla pudding
1 (15.25 oz.) can sliced peaches (drain and reserve juice)
12 oz. cream cheese
1 cup sugar
4 tablespoons peach juice

Preheat oven to 350 degrees F. Mix yellow cake mix per package instructions. Add flour and pudding mix. Pour into a greased 13x9x2" baking dish. Arrange peach slices on top of batter. Mix cream cheese, sugar and peach juice. Put this mixture on top of peaches. Bake at 350 degrees F for 50 to 60 minutes or until cake springs back when lightly touched.

Peach, Coconut, Nut Dessert

1 (29 oz.) can sliced peaches
1 box butter pecan cake mix
1/2 cup butter or margarine, melted
1 cup coconut, shredded
1/2 to 1 cup pecans, chopped

Preheat oven to 325 degrees F. Layer in an ungreased 13x9x2-inch baking dish, peaches, cake mix, melted butter (drizzled over cake mix), coconut and chopped pecans. Bake at 325 degrees F for 50 to 60 minutes. Let stand 15 to 20 minutes before serving. Serve topped with vanilla ice cream.

Apple Desert

1 (20 oz.) can apple pie filling
1/2 package cake mix, white or yellow
1/2 cup butter or margarine
1/2 cup slivered almonds or walnuts
Cinnamon, as desired

Preheat oven to 350 degrees F. Cover bottom of 9x9x2" pan with pie filling. Sprinkle with cinnamon. Sprinkle cake mix over pie filling. Cut butter into squares and place over cake mix. Sprinkle slivered almonds over top. Bake 30 to 45 minutes at 350 degrees F or until brown. Serve with ice cream or plain. If desired, recipe may be doubled using larger pan.

Yield: 8 servings.

Pumpkin Dessert

1 (30 oz.) can pumpkin
1 (12 oz.) can evaporated milk
3 eggs, slightly beaten
1/2 teaspoon salt
1 cup sugar
1 1/2 teaspoons cinnamon
1/4 teaspoon cloves
1/4 teaspoon ginger
1/2 teaspoon nutmeg
1 yellow cake mix
3/4 cup butter
Walnuts

Preheat oven to 350 degrees F. In a large bowl, combine all ingredients except cake mix and butter. Pour mixture into greased 13x9x2-inch baking dish. Sprinkle dry cake mix on top. Melt butter and pour over cake mix. Place broken walnuts on top. Bake at 350 degrees F for 50 to 60 minutes, until set.

Cherry Pie Filling Cake

1 (16.5 oz.) package yellow cake mix
5 tablespoons + 1 teaspoon flour
2 eggs
1 tablespoon vegetable oil
1 (21 oz.) can cherry pie filling

Topping:

1/2 cup brown sugar, packed
1/2 cup nuts, chopped

Preheat oven to 350 degrees F. In a large bowl, combine cake mix, flour, eggs and oil. Add cherry pie filling. Spread in 10 1/2 x 15 1/2 x 1" jelly roll pan sprayed with nonstick cooking spray. Combine brown sugar and nuts and sprinkle on top of cake. Bake 30 minutes at 350 degrees F.

Chocolate Cakes

Sweet Chocolate Cake

1 package German chocolate cake mix
8 oz. cream cheese, softened
2 cups chocolate chips
2 teaspoons vanilla
1 cup sugar
2 eggs
1 cup pecans

Preheat oven to 350 degrees F. Prepare cake mix according to directions. Pour into 13x9x2" baking dish and set aside. In a large bowl, combine cream cheese, chocolate chips, vanilla, sugar, eggs and pecans and drop by teaspoonfuls on cake batter. Bake at 350 degrees F for 40 to 50 minutes. Frost when cooled.

Frosting:

1 (3 oz.) package instant chocolate pudding
1 package Dream Whip (dry)
1 1/2 cups milk
1 teaspoon vanilla

Combine all ingredients and whip together until thick. Spread on cooled cake. Refrigerate, covered.

Hot Brownie Pudding Cake

1 (16.5 oz.) package devil's food cake mix
5 tablespoons + 1 teaspoon flour
1 cup walnuts, chopped
1 cup brown sugar, packed
1/4 cup cocoa powder
1 3/4 cups hot water

Preheat oven to 350 degrees F. Combine cake mix and flour. Prepare cake as directed on package. Pour 1/2 of batter into greased 9-inch square pan, (use remaining half for cupcakes). Combine walnuts, brown sugar and cocoa powder. Sprinkle walnut mixture over batter. Pour hot water over all. Bake at 350 degrees F for 45 minutes. Serve warm with ice cream or whipped cream.

Snicker Cake

1 package German chocolate cake mix
1 (14 oz.) package caramels
1/4 cup margarine
1/3 cup milk
3/4 cup chocolate chips
1 cup pecans

Preheat oven to 350 degrees F. Prepare cake mix according to package directions. Pour 1/2 of the batter in a 13x9x2" baking dish; bake at 350 degrees F for 20 minutes.

In microwave, melt caramels, margarine, and milk stirring every 30 seconds until smooth. Pour over baked cake. Top with chocolate chips and pecans, then dot remaining batter over all. Reduce heat to 250 degrees F and bake for 20 minutes. Then increase heat to 350 degrees F and bake for 10 to 15 minutes. Serve with refrigerated whipped topping or ice cream.

5-Cup Cake

1 package chocolate cake mix
1 (14 oz.) can sweetened condensed milk
1 (12.25 oz.) jar caramel topping
1 (16 oz.) carton refrigerated whipped topping
1 (1.4 oz.) Heath candy bar, crushed

Bake the cake according to directions. After it has cooled, poke holes in the top with the end of a wooden spoon. Pour the can of condensed milk over the top, then the jar of topping. Frost with whipped topping and then sprinkle the top with the crushed candy bar.

Chocolate Chip Cake

1 (16.5 oz.) package chocolate cake mix
5 tablespoons + 1 teaspoon flour
1 (3.4 oz.) box cook & serve chocolate pudding
1 (12 oz.) package milk chocolate chips

Preheat oven to 350 degrees F. Cook pudding as per directions on box (to boil). In a large bowl, combine cake mix, flour and pudding. Pour into greased 13x9x2" baking dish. Spread chocolate chips over top. Bake at 350 degrees F for 35 to 45 minutes or until tests clean with toothpick. Let cool.

Earthquake Cake

1 cup coconut
1 cup pecans
1 (16.5 oz.) package chocolate cake mix
5 tablespoons + 1 teaspoon flour
1 cup margarine, melted
1 (8 oz.) package cream cheese, softened
1 (16 oz.) box confectioners' sugar

Preheat oven to 325 degrees F. In a 13x9x2" baking dish, layer coconut and pecans. Combine cake mix and flour. Sprinkle dry cake mix mixture on top. Combine margarine, cream cheese and confectioners' sugar. Spread on top of cake mix. (Bake cake with a sheet of aluminum foil under it in case it bubbles over.) Bake at 325 degrees F for 1 hour.

Chocolate Zucchini Cake

1 (16.5 oz.) package dark chocolate cake mix
5 tablespoons + 1 teaspoon flour
1 teaspoon cinnamon
3 eggs
1 1/4 cups water
1/2 cup vegetable oil
1 cup zucchini, shredded and unpeeled
Can of vanilla frosting
1/4 cup pecans, chopped

Preheat oven to 350 degrees F. Grease and flour a 10" tube pan. Combine dry cake mix, flour and cinnamon in a large bowl. Add eggs, water and oil; mix well. With an electric mixer, beat for 2 minutes at medium speed. Mix in zucchini. Pour batter into pan and spread evenly. Bake at 350 degrees F for 50 to 60 minutes. Cool completely before removing from pan. When fully cool, frost with vanilla frosting and sprinkle pecans over the top.

Twinkie Cake

1 (16.5 oz.) package chocolate cake mix

Filling:

5 tablespoons flour
1 cup milk
1 cup sugar
1/2 teaspoon salt
1/2 cup vegetable oil
1/2 cup butter
1 teaspoon vanilla

Frosting:

1/2 cup butter
1/2 cup milk
2 cups sugar
1 cup chocolate chips
2 teaspoons vanilla

Bake chocolate cake mix in 13x9x2" baking dish according to package directions. With a long piece of sewing thread, starting at one end of cake, pull thread tight and use thread to cut cake through center from one end to the other. Remove top layer carefully. Frost bottom half with filling (see below). Replace top layer and frost.

Filling: Cook flour and milk in a saucepan on medium to

high heat until mixture thickens; cool. Add remaining ingredients to cooled flour mixture and whip on high until texture of whipped cream.

Frosting: In a medium saucepan, bring butter, milk and sugar to a boil. Remove from heat. Add chocolate chips and vanilla. Let cool until spreading consistency.

The Best Chocolate Cake

1 (16.5 oz.) package chocolate cake mix
1 (14 oz.) can sweetened condensed milk
1 (6 oz.) caramel or hot fudge sauce
1 (8 oz.) refrigerated whipped topping
2 Skor (1.4 oz.) candy bars, crushed

In a large bowl, mix cake mix according to directions. Bake according to package instructions in a 13x9x2" baking dish. Pierce warm cake all over with toothpick. Pour sweetened condensed milk over cake. Pour caramel or hot fudge sauce over cake. Chill. Before serving, top with refrigerated whipped topping and top with crushed Skor candy bars.

Almond Joy Cake

1 (16.5 oz.) package chocolate cake mix
1 (14 oz.) can sweetened condensed milk
2 (3 1/2 oz.) cans coconut
1 (13.5 oz.) can cream of coconut
1 (12 oz.) carton refrigerated whipped topping

Bake cake mix as directed on box in a 13x9x2" baking dish. Poke holes in top of cake with handle of a wooden spoon while cake is still hot. Immediately, pour can of sweetened condensed milk and 1/2 can cream of coconut over top of cake. Top with 1 can coconut; cool. Then, top with whipped topping. Top with one can of coconut. For Easter, sprinkle top with jellybeans and tint coconut in different colors.

Turtle Cake

1 (16.5 oz.) package German chocolate cake mix
1 (14 oz.) package caramels (or 1 cup caramel dip)
1/2 (14 oz.) can Eagle Brand sweetened condensed milk
1/2 cup margarine
1 cup chocolate chips
1 cup nuts
Can of coconut pecan frosting

Mix cake as directed on package. Pour half of batter into greased and floured 13x9x2" baking dish. Bake at 350 degrees F for 15 minutes. Melt caramels, milk, and margarine in a double boiler; pour over baked cake. Sprinkle chocolate chips and nuts over cake. Pour remaining batter onto cake; bake at 350 degrees F for 20 minutes. Top with coconut pecan frosting.

Triple Chocolate Cake

1 (16.5 oz.) package chocolate cake mix
5 tablespoons + 1 teaspoon flour
1 (3.9 oz.) box chocolate instant pudding
1 3/4 cups milk
2 eggs
12 oz. semi-sweet chocolate chips

Preheat oven to 350 degrees F. In a large bowl, mix cake mix, flour, pudding, milk and eggs with electric mixer at medium speed until well combined. Stir in chocolate chips. Pour into well-greased and floured 13x9x2" baking dish. Bake at 350 degrees F for 50 to 55 minutes. Cool 15 minutes. Sprinkle, if desired, with confectioners' sugar just before serving.

Ho-Ho Cake

1 package chocolate cake mix
1 1/4 cups milk
5 tablespoons flour
1 teaspoon vanilla
1/2 cup butter or margarine, softened
1/2 cup vegetable oil
1 cup sugar

Preheat oven to 350 degrees F. Prepare chocolate cake mix as directed on package and bake in jellyroll pan at 350 degrees F for 20 to 25 minutes.

In a saucepan, combine milk, flour and vanilla and boil until thick. Set aside to cool. Beat butter or margarine, oil and sugar together. Add cooled flour mixture, beat until fluffy. Spread on cake and refrigerate 1 hour.

Frosting:

1/2 cup butter or margarine
4 tablespoons cocoa
6 to 7 tablespoons milk
1 lb. box confectioners' sugar
1 teaspoon vanilla
In a saucepan, combine margarine, cocoa and milk; bring to a boil. Remove from heat and add confectioners' sugar and vanilla. Frost cake immediately.

CAKES

Cakes

Ricotta Cake

1 (16.5 oz.) package yellow cake mix
5 tablespoons + 1 teaspoon flour
2 lbs. Ricotta cheese
4 eggs
1 cup sugar
1 teaspoon vanilla
Confectioners' sugar

Preheat oven to 350 degrees F. Prepare cake mix as directed on package, add flour and mix well. Pour into a greased and floured 13x9x2" baking dish.

In a large bowl, combine Ricotta cheese, eggs, sugar and vanilla and beat until smooth and blended; pour over the yellow cake mix batter. Bake at 350 degrees F for one hour or until golden brown and set in center. Dust with confectioners' sugar when cool.

Two Ingredient Cake

1 (15.25 oz.) package yellow cake mix
12 ounces lemon-lime soda

Combine the two ingredients and bake as directed on the cake mix box. Cool and frost with canned frosting or a favorite frosting recipe.

Variations:

Orange cake mix with lemon-lime soda or vanilla cream soda

White cake mix with orange soda

Chocolate cake mix with Dr. Pepper or Cherry Coke

Strawberry cake mix with lemon-lime soda

Note: Use only the 2 ingredients listed, not any additional ingredients that may be on the cake box.

This cake will not rise quite as much as a regular box cake, and it won't win a blue ribbon at the fair, but it is fun, quick to make and tastes good. Try the recipe with cupcakes too.

Coconut Gem Cake

1 (16.5 oz.) package yellow cake mix
5 tablespoons + 1 teaspoon flour
2 1/2 cups coconut
1 (16 oz.) can fruit cocktail with syrup
2 eggs
1/2 cup brown sugar, packed
1/2 cup butter
1/2 cup sugar
1/2 cup evaporated milk

Preheat oven to 325 degrees F. In a large bowl, combine cake mix, flour, 1 cup coconut, fruit cocktail and eggs; mix well. Pour into greased and floured 13x9x2" baking dish, sprinkle with brown sugar. Bake at 325 degrees F for 45 minutes.

In a saucepan, bring butter, sugar and milk to a boil and boil for 2 minutes. Remove mixture from heat and stir in remaining 1 1/2 cups coconut. Spoon over hot cake in pan.

Gooey Butter Cake

1 (16.5 oz.) package yellow cake mix
5 tablespoons + 1 teaspoon flour
1/2 cup margarine or butter, melted
4 eggs
1 (8 oz.) package cream cheese, softened
1 (1 lb.) package confectioners' sugar

Preheat oven to 350 degrees F. In a large bowl, combine cake mix, flour, margarine or butter and 2 eggs by hand. Spread into greased 13x9x2" baking dish; set aside.

Mix 2 eggs, confectioners' sugar and cream cheese together with electric mixer at medium speed, until well combined. Pour over cake mix mixture. Bake at 350 degrees F for 35 to 40 minutes.

Pistachio Cake

1 (16.5 oz.) package yellow cake mix
5 tablespoons + 1 teaspoon flour
1 cup club soda
1/2 cup nuts, optional
4 eggs
1 (3.4 oz.) box instant pistachio pudding

Preheat oven to 350 degrees F. Mix all ingredients together in a large bowl and pour into greased and floured 13x9x2" baking dish. Bake at 350 degrees F for 35 to 40 minutes.

Frosting:

1 (12 oz.) carton refrigerated whipped topping
1 (3.4 oz.) box instant pistachio pudding

Mix together and spread on cooled cake.

1950's Cake

1 (16.5 oz.) package yellow cake mix
5 tablespoons + 1 teaspoon flour
1 (4 oz.) package instant vanilla pudding
4 eggs
3/4 cup vegetable oil
3/4 cup sherry
1 teaspoon nutmeg

Preheat oven to 350 degrees F. In a large bowl, combine all ingredients; beat for 5 minutes at medium speed. Pour into a greased 10" tube cake pan or mold and bake for 45 minutes at 350 degrees F.

Apricot Nectar Cake

1 (16.5 oz.) package lemon cake mix
5 tablespoons + 1 teaspoon flour
3/4 cup vegetable oil or canola oil
4 eggs
2 teaspoons lemon extract (optional)
6 oz. apricot nectar

Preheat oven to 350 degrees F. Combine all ingredients in a large bowl and beat with electric mixer at medium speed for 1 minute. Bake in greased tube pan at 350 degrees F for 45 minutes.

Topping:

Juice of 2 lemons
1/2 box confectioners' sugar

Mix lemon juice and confectioners' sugar together and spread on cake while still warm.

Wine Cake

1 (16.5 oz.) package lemon cake mix
5 tablespoons + 1 teaspoon flour
1 (3.4 oz.) package instant vanilla pudding
1 teaspoon nutmeg
4 eggs
3/4 cup wine
3/4 cup vegetable oil

Preheat oven to 350 degrees F. Combine all ingredients in a large bowl and beat for 5 minutes. Grease large angel food cake pan and dust with flour. Pour mixture in pan and bake at 350 degrees F for 45 to 60 minutes. Cool in pan 5 minutes. Remove from pan and dust with confectioners' sugar.

Audubon German Torte

1 package yellow cake mix

Torte filling:

3 tablespoons cornstarch
1/3 cup sugar
1/8 teaspoon salt
1 cup milk
1 egg, beaten
1/2 teaspoon vanilla
3 egg whites
1/ 4 cup sugar
1 teaspoon margarine

1 (21 oz.) can cherry pie filling

Prepare cake mix according to directions. Bake in two 9-inch layer pans.

To make torte filling: Combine cornstarch, sugar and salt in double boiler. Add milk and egg. Cook over boiling water, stirring constantly until thickened. Stir in vanilla and margarine. Allow to cool. Make meringue by beating the 3 egg whites very stiff, gradually adding the 1/4 cup of sugar.

Place foil on a cookie sheet and place a cake layer on foil, spread the torte filling on cake layer. Place second layer on top. Spread meringue around edge of cake, making ridge around top. Spread a thin layer of meringue on top. Brown meringue for about 10 minutes at 425 degrees F or until nicely browned. Spoon cherry filling on top.

Hershey Bar Cake

1 (16.5 oz.) package white cake mix
5 tablespoons + 1 teaspoon flour
2 eggs
1/2 cup vegetable oil
1 (14 oz.) can sweetened condensed milk
1/2 cup butter or margarine
1 1/2 (7 oz.) Hershey bars (large)

Preheat oven to 350 degrees F. In a large bowl, combine cake mix, flour, oil and eggs with spoon until blended. Melt margarine, condensed milk and Hershey bar in microwave on 1/2 power for 5 to 10 minutes until chocolate is melted. Press 1/2 of cake mixture in 13x9x2" baking dish. Pour chocolate mix on top of cake mixture. Using remaining cake mix, place small size pieces on chocolate. Bake at 350 degrees F for 25 to 30 minutes. Cool before cutting.

Pilgrim Cake

1 (16.5 oz.) package spice cake mix
5 tablespoons + 1 teaspoon flour
1 (16 oz.) can pumpkin
2 eggs
2 teaspoons baking soda
1/3 cup water
1/2 pint whipping cream
1/4 cup brown sugar, packed
1 teaspoon vanilla
Maraschino cherries

Preheat oven to 350 degrees F. In a large bowl, beat cake mix, flour, pumpkin, eggs, baking soda, and water together. Bake in a greased and floured 13x9x2" baking dish at 350 degrees F for 45 minutes. Whip cream with brown sugar and vanilla to top each piece when serving. Garnish each serving with a maraschino cherry.

Yield: 12 to 15 servings.

Coconut Sheet Cake

1 (16.5 oz.) package yellow cake mix
1 (13 oz.) carton refrigerated whipped topping

Syrup:
1 (14 oz.) package coconut
1 cup sugar
2 cups milk

Prepare cake according to package directions. Pour into two 8-inch square baking dishes and microwave one at a time on 50% power 6 minutes, then HIGH 2 to 6 minutes until done. Let stand 10 minutes on countertop.

Meanwhile prepare the syrup. Combine syrup ingredients and microwave on HIGH 5 to 6 minutes or to boiling. Stir to dissolve sugar. Poke holes in cake with a fork and pour syrup over. Cool 30 minutes. Spread whipped topping over cake and refrigerate overnight or longer before serving.

Yield: 2 8-inch squares.

Quick Red Velvet Cake

1 (16.5 oz.) package yellow cake mix
5 tablespoons + 1 teaspoon flour
5 eggs
2 tablespoons cocoa powder
1/2 cup vegetable oil
1 cup low-fat buttermilk
(2 oz.) red food coloring

Frosting:

1 (8 oz.) package cream cheese
2 cups confectioners' sugar
1/2 cup butter or margarine, softened
1 teaspoon vanilla

In a large bowl, combine cake mix, flour, eggs, cocoa powder, oil, buttermilk and food coloring. Mix until well blended. Bake according to directions on cake mix package.

Frosting: In a medium bowl, mix all frosting ingredients. Spread frosting when cake is cooled slightly.

Boston Cream Cheese Cake

1 (9 oz.) package yellow cake mix
2 (8 oz.) pkgs. cream cheese (softened)
1/2 cup granulated sugar
1 teaspoon vanilla
2 eggs
1/3 cup sour cream
2 tablespoons cold water
2 (1 oz.) square unsweetened chocolate
3 tablespoons margarine
1 cup confectioners' sugar
1 teaspoon vanilla

Preheat oven to 350 degrees F. Grease bottom of 9-inch springform pan. Prepare cake mix as directed on package; pour batter into pan and bake at 350 degrees F for 20 minutes. In a large bowl, combine cream cheese, sugar and vanilla; mix at medium speed with electric mixer until well mixed.

Add eggs 1 at a time, blending after each addition. Mix in sour cream; pour over cake layer. Bake at 350 degrees F for 35 minutes. Loosen cake from rim of pan; cool before removing rim of pan. Bring water to boil; remove from heat. Melt chocolate with margarine over low heat, stirring until smooth. Remove from heat. Add water and remaining ingredients; mix well. Spread over cheese cake; chill several hours. Garnish with strawberries.

Marbled Pistachio Cake

1 (16.5 oz.) package lemon cake mix
5 tablespoons + 1 teaspoon flour
1 (3.4 oz.) package jello pistachio instant pudding
1 cup water
4 eggs
1/2 cup vegetable oil
1/2 teaspoon almond extract
1/4 cup chocolate syrup

Preheat oven to 350 degrees F. Combine cake mix, flour, pudding, water, eggs, oil and almond extract in large bowl; mix well. With electric mixer, beat at medium speed for 2 minutes.

Pour one-third of batter into another bowl; mix in chocolate syrup. Alternately pour batters into greased and floured 10" tube pan. Using a knife, zigzag through the batter to marble. Bake at 350 degrees F for 50 minutes, or until center springs back when lightly touched. Cool in pan for 15 minutes.

Crème De Menthe Cake

1 package white cake mix
3 teaspoons crème de menthe
1 (12.8 oz.) jar hot fudge ice cream topping
3 teaspoons (or more to taste) crème de menthe
1 (8 oz.) carton refrigerated whipped topping

Prepare cake mix as directed on package. Add crème de menthe, should be light green in color. Bake as directed on package and cool. When cool, spread hot fudge ice cream topping over cake. Mix crème de menthe with refrigerated whipped topping. Spread over fudge topping. Store in refrigerator.

BARS

Bars

Lemon Chocolate Bars

1 (16.5 oz.) package chocolate cake mix
5 tablespoons + 1 teaspoon flour
1 (3.4 oz.) box instant lemon pudding
1 (8.5 oz.) can fruit cocktail, juice and all
4 beaten eggs
1/4 cup vegetable oil

Preheat oven to 350 degrees F. In a large bowl, combine all ingredients. Bake on a sheet cake pan at 350 degrees F for 30 minutes or until done. Frost when cool.

Yield: 36 bars.

Chocolate Turtle Bars

1 (16.5 oz.) package German chocolate cake mix
5 tablespoons + 1 teaspoon flour
3/4 cup margarine, melted
1 cup nuts
1 (14 oz.) package caramels
1 cup chocolate chips
1 cup (5 1/4 oz.) evaporated milk

Preheat oven to 350 degrees F. In a medium saucepan, combine caramels and 1/3 cup evaporated milk. Cook over low heat until melted.

In a large bowl, combine cake mix, flour, margarine, 1/3 cup evaporated milk. Fold in nuts. Stir by hand until dough holds together (fudge-like consistency). Spread half dough in 13x9x2" baking dish. Bake at 350 degrees F for 6 minutes. Remove from oven. Sprinkle with chocolate chips. Drizzle melted caramels over chips. Dot rest of cake dough over top. Bake at 350 degrees F for 20 minutes. Cool slightly before cutting into bars.

Yield: 30 to 36 bars.

Pumpkin Pie Squares

1 package yellow cake mix
1/2 cup butter or margarine, melted
1 egg

Filling:
3 cups (1 lb. 14 oz.) can pumpkin pie mix
2 eggs
2/3 cup milk

Topping:
1 cup reserved cake mix
1/4 cup sugar
1 teaspoon cinnamon
1/4 cup butter or margarine

Preheat oven to 350 degrees F. Spray bottom only of a 13x9x2" baking dish with non-stick cooking spray. Reserve 1 cup of cake mix for topping. Mix together remaining cake mix, butter or margarine and egg. Press into pan.

Filling: In a large bowl, combine pumpkin pie mix, 2 eggs and 2/3 cup milk. Mix until smooth. Pour mixture over crust.

Topping: Combine topping ingredients; sprinkle over filling. Bake at 350 degrees F for 45 to 50 minutes until knife inserted near center comes out clean. If desired, top with whipped cream. Yield: 30 bars.

Salted Nut Roll Candy Bars

1 (16.5 oz.) package yellow cake mix
5 tablespoons + 1 teaspoon flour
2/3 cup margarine, melted
1 egg
3 cups mini marshmallows
2/3 cup white corn syrup
1/2 cup margarine
2 teaspoons vanilla
1 (12 oz.) package peanut butter chips

Topping:

1 cup crispy rice cereal
1 cup salted peanuts

Preheat oven to 350 degrees F. In a large bowl, combine cake mix, flour, 2/3 cup melted margarine and egg; mix well. Pat into 13x9x2" baking dish. Bake at 350 degrees F for 12 to 15 minutes. Place marshmallows on top; return to oven until marshmallows puff up.

In a medium saucepan, combine corn syrup, 1/2 cup margarine, peanut butter chips and vanilla. Melt over medium heat; mix well. Pour over marshmallows.

Topping: Combine cereal and peanuts. Arrange on top and slightly press into syrup mixture. Refrigerate.

Yield: 30 to 36 bars.

Chess Squares

1 (16.5 oz.) package yellow cake mix
5 tablespoons + 1 teaspoon flour
3 eggs
1/2 cup margarine
1/4 teaspoon salt
1/2 teaspoon vanilla
3 cups confectioners' sugar
1 (8 oz.) package cream cheese

Preheat oven to 325 degrees F. In a large bowl, combine cake mix, 1 egg, and margarine; mix well. Put in 13x9x2" baking dish. Beat remaining 2 eggs, salt, vanilla, confectioners' sugar, and cream cheese together for 3 minutes. Pour over first layer. Bake at 325 degrees F for 35 to 45 minutes.

Yield: 30 to 36 bars.

Chocolate Chip Butterscotch Bars

1 (16.5 oz.) package yellow cake mix
5 tablespoons + 1 teaspoon flour
2 eggs
1/2 cup vegetable oil or canola oil
1 (3.4 oz.) box instant butterscotch pudding mix
1 cup flaked coconut
1 (6 oz.) small package chocolate chips
1 cup pecans

Preheat oven to 350 degrees F. In a large bowl, beat eggs. Add oil, cake mix, flour and pudding mix. Stir in coconut, chocolate chips and nuts. Put in greased 13x9x2" baking dish and bake 25 to 35 minutes at 350 degrees F.

Yield: 36 bars.

Caramel Bars

1 (14 oz.) package caramels
2/3 cup evaporated milk (divided)
1 (16.5 oz.) package German chocolate cake mix
5 tablespoons + 1 teaspoon flour
3/4 cup margarine, melted
2 cups chocolate chips

Preheat oven to 350 degrees F. In a double boiler or microwave-safe dish, combine caramels and 1/3 cup evaporated milk. Cook, stirring occasionally until caramels are melted. In a large bowl, mix together cake mix, flour, margarine and 1/3 cup evaporated milk. Pat 1/2 of cake mixture into a greased 13x9x2" baking dish. Bake at 350 degrees F for 7 minutes.

Remove from oven and sprinkle with 2 cup chocolate chips over dough. Pour caramel mixture on top. Spread remaining cake dough mixture over top of caramel. Bake at 350 degrees F for 18 to 20 minutes longer.

Yield: 30 bars.

Lemon Cheese Bars

1 (16.5 oz.) package yellow cake mix
5 tablespoons + 1 teaspoon flour
1 egg
1/3 cup vegetable oil

Preheat oven to 350 degrees F. Mix cake mix, flour, egg and oil until crumbly. Pat all but 1 cup of mixture lightly in an ungreased 13x9x2" baking dish. Bake at 350 degrees F for 15 minutes. Remove from oven. Have filling ready.

Filling:

1 (8 oz.) package cream cheese
1/3 cup sugar
1 egg
1/4 cup lemon juice
Beat all ingredients together until light and smooth. Spread over baked layer while hot. Sprinkle with reserved crumb mixture. Bake for 15 minutes longer. Cool and cut into bars.

Yield: 30 bars.

Macaroon Cookie Bars

1 package devil's food or dark chocolate cake mix
1 egg
1/3 cup margarine or butter, softened
1 (14 oz.) can sweetened condensed milk
1 teaspoon vanilla
1 egg
1 cup pecans, chopped
1 1/4 cups coconut

Preheat oven to 350 degrees F. Spray a 13x9x2" baking dish with non-stick cooking spray. In a large bowl, combine cake mix, egg and margarine or butter. With electric mixer, mix at highest speed until crumbly. Press firmly into bottom of baking dish.

In a small bowl, beat sweetened condensed milk, vanilla and egg until well mixed. Mix in pecans and 1 cup coconut. Pour over cake mixture in baking dish, spread to cover. Sprinkle remaining 1/4 cup coconut over top. Bake at 350 degrees F for 30 to 40 minutes or until golden brown. Center may appear loose but will set upon cooling. Cool completely before cutting.

Yield: 36 bars.

Yellow Pecan Bars or Cake

1/2 cup butter or margarine, softened
1 (16.5 oz.) package yellow cake mix
5 tablespoons + 1 teaspoon flour
1 cup pecans, chopped (opt.)
1 teaspoon vanilla
4 eggs, divided
1 box (1 lb.) confectioners' sugar
1 (8 oz.) package cream cheese, softened

Preheat oven to 325 degrees F. Combine butter or margarine, yellow cake mix, flour, pecans, vanilla and 1 egg in a large bowl. Pat into large baking pan with sides (like a jellyroll pan), helps to scatter small teaspoonfuls over pan before patting. Mix together cream cheese, confectioners' sugar and 3 eggs. Pour over batter in pan. Bake at 325 degrees F for 30 to 40 minutes, or until golden brown. Let cool for 1 to 2 hours before cutting into squares.

Variation: For more of a cake-type dessert, grease and flour a 13x9x2" baking dish and bake at 300 degrees F for 1 hour. When done, sprinkle with additional confectioners' sugar, if desired.

Yield: 30 squares.

Filled Chocolate Bars

1 (16.5 oz.) package chocolate cake mix

Preheat oven to 350 degrees F. Mix cake mix as directed on package. Pour onto a cookie sheet sprayed with non-stick cooking spray. Bake 20 minutes at 350 degrees F. Cool.

Filling:

3/4 cup sugar
2/3 cup vegetable oil
1 (5 oz.) can evaporated milk
1/2 cup butter or margarine, melted
1/8 teaspoon salt
1 1/2 teaspoons vanilla
In a large bowl, combine all filling ingredients; beat until fluffy. Spread on cooled cake.

Topping:

1 can milk chocolate frosting

Warm can of frosting and spread on top of cake. (Microwave for 35 seconds.) Cool and serve.

Yield: 30 to 36 bars.

Lemon Squares

1 (16.5 oz.) package lemon chiffon or white angel food cake mix
1 (6 oz.) package lemon flavored gelatin
2 cups boiling water
1 (6 oz.) can frozen lemonade concentrate, thawed
1 1/2 cups whipping cream
1/2 cup flaked coconut

Bake cake as directed on package; let cool. In a large bowl, combine gelatin and boiling water; stir until gelatin is dissolved. Refrigerate until thickened but not set.

Add enough cold water to thawed lemonade concentrate to make 2 cups; stir lemonade into gelatin. Beat until foamy.

In a large chilled bowl, beat whipping cream until stiff; fold into gelatin. Tear cake into 1 inch pieces. Add cake pieces to gelatin mixture. Spread in 13x9x2" baking dish; sprinkle with coconut. Refrigerate until firm, at least 4 hours. Cut into squares.

Yield: 30 to 36 bars.

Cookie Bars

1 (16.5 oz.) package yellow cake mix
5 tablespoons + 1 teaspoon flour
1/2 cup butter
1 egg
1 (8 oz.) package cream cheese
1 1/2 cups sugar
1 teaspoon vanilla
1 egg
Nuts, chopped

Preheat oven to 350 degrees F. Combine cake mix, flour, butter and egg in a large bowl. Pat into a 10 1/2 x 15-inch jelly roll pan.

In a medium bowl, mix cream cheese, sugar, vanilla and egg together. Spread on top of cookie sheet pan and top with nuts. Bake at 350 degrees F for 30 to 35 minutes.

Yield: 30 to 36 bars.

Peanut Butter Chocolate Chip Bars

1 (16.5 oz.) package yellow cake mix
5 tablespoons + 1 teaspoon flour
2 eggs
1/3 cup vegetable oil
1/2 cup chunky peanut butter
1 cup chocolate chips

Preheat oven to 350 degrees F. In a large bowl, combine cake mix, flour, eggs and oil. Stir in peanut butter. Stir in chocolate chips. Pat mixture into a 13x9x2" baking dish. Bake at 350 degrees F for 14 to 17 minutes or until golden brown.

Yield: 30 to 36 bars.

Deluxe Chocolate Marshmallow Bars

1 package chocolate cake mix
1/2 cup nuts (opt.)
4 cups miniature marshmallows
1 1/3 cups chocolate chips
3 tablespoons margarine
1 cup peanut butter
2 cups crispy rice cereal

Prepare cake mix according to directions, adding nuts if desired. Pour into a greased jellyroll pan and bake according to package instructions. Top with marshmallows and bake for an additional 2 to 4 minutes. Spread the marshmallows evenly over the cake with a knife dipped in cold water. (Dip the knife frequently to prevent sticking.) Allow the bars to cool.

In a saucepan, melt the chocolate chips, margarine and peanut butter. Stir over low heat until combined. Remove from heat and add cereal. Spread over cooled bars.

Yield: 36 bars.

Cherry Brownie Bars

1 (16.5 oz.) package chocolate cake mix
5 tablespoons + 1 teaspoon flour
1 (21 oz.) can cherry pie filling
2 eggs

In a large bowl, combine all ingredients. Mix together at medium speed for 5 minutes. Bake at 350 degrees F for 35 to 40 minutes. Frost when cool.

Yield: 30 to 36 bars.

Rich Chocolate Chip Bars

1 (16.5 oz.) package white cake mix
2 large eggs
1/3 cup vegetable oil
1 (14 oz.) can sweetened condensed milk
1 (6 oz.) package semi-sweet chocolate chips
1/2 cup butter or margarine, cut small

Preheat oven to 350 degrees F. Spray a 13x9x2" baking dish with non-stick cooking spray. Beat cake mix, eggs and oil in a large bowl with mixer at medium speed until well blended. Press two-thirds into baking dish.

Microwave condensed milk, chocolate chips and butter in a bowl on high 1 minute or until mixture is smooth when stirred. Pour into baking dish over cake mixture. Top with teaspoonfuls of reserved cake mixture. Bake at 350 degrees F for 20 to 25 minutes until lightly browned. Cool; cut into bars.

Yield: 48 bars.

Nutty Cheese Bars

1 (16.5 oz.) package classic butter golden cake mix
1 1/2 cups pecans or walnuts, chopped
3/4 cup margarine, melted
2 (8 oz. each) packages cream cheese, softened
1 cup brown sugar, packed

Preheat oven to 350 degrees F. Combine cake mix, 3/4 cup chopped nuts and margarine. Press into 9x13x2-inch greased and floured baking dish.

In another bowl, combine cream cheese and brown sugar until well mixed. Spread over cake mixture and sprinkle with remaining nuts.

Bake at 350 degrees F for 25 to 30 minutes. Cool and refrigerate.

Yield: 30 to 36 bars.

Chewy Pecan Pie Squares

1 yellow cake mix
1/3 cup vegetable oil
5 eggs
1 cup maple syrup
1 cup sugar
1/4 cup margarine or butter, melted
2 cups (8 oz.) pecans

Preheat oven to 350 degrees F. Grease a 13x9x2" baking dish. In a large bowl, combine cake mix, oil and 1 egg until crumbly. Press into baking dish; bake 20 minutes.

Beat remaining eggs with syrup, sugar and margarine or butter until well mixed. Stir in pecans. Pour on top of hot crust. Bake at 350 degrees F for 40 minutes or until filling has set. Cool completely. Cut into squares.

Yield: 30 to 36 bars.

Lemon Bars

1 (16.5 oz.) package yellow cake mix
5 tablespoons + 1 teaspoon flour
1 (3 oz.) box lemon jello
4 eggs
3/4 cup water

Glaze:
2 cups confectioners' sugar
1/3 cup lemon juice
Enough water to spread easily

In a large bowl, combine cake mix, flour, jello, eggs and water; beat for 4 minutes. Bake as directed on package in a 13x9x2" baking dish.

When done, take a fork and poke holes all over cake. Combine all glaze ingredients and spread glaze on cake.

Yield: 30 to 36 bars.

Streusels

Coffee Cake

1 (16.5 oz.) package yellow cake mix
5 tablespoons + 1 teaspoon flour
1 (3.4 oz.) package instant vanilla pudding
3/4 cup vegetable oil
3/4 cup water
4 eggs
1 teaspoon vanilla

Topping:

1/4 cup granulated sugar
1/3 cup brown sugar, packed
1 1/2 teaspoons cinnamon
1/2 cup pecans, chopped

Preheat oven to 350 degrees F. In a large bowl, combine cake mix, flour and pudding. In another bowl, mix oil, water, eggs and vanilla; add to cake mix mixture. Pour half of cake mix mixture into a 13x9x2" greased baking dish.

In a medium bowl, combine all topping ingredients. Sprinkle half the topping over the cake mixture in baking dish. Pour the rest of the cake mix mixture in baking dish; sprinkle the rest of the topping mixture. Bake at 350 degrees F for 40 minutes.

Cinnamon Streusel Coffee Cake

1 (16.5 oz.) package yellow cake mix
5 tablespoons + 1 teaspoon flour
1 (3.4 oz.) box vanilla instant pudding
2 tablespoons vegetable oil
1 1/2 cups cooled coffee
2 eggs
1/4 cup flour
1/4 cup brown sugar, packed
1/2 teaspoon cinnamon
1 tablespoon margarine or butter, softened

Preheat oven to 350 degrees F. In a large bowl, blend cake mix, 5 tablespoons + 1 teaspoon flour, pudding, oil, coffee and eggs. Beat 2 minutes at medium speed. Spread batter evenly in greased and floured 10-inch tube pan.

Combine flour, brown sugar and cinnamon. Add butter and mix. Sprinkle over batter and bake at 350 degrees F for 40 to 50 minutes. Remove to wire rack to cool, streusel side up.

Yield: 12 to 16 servings.

Graham Streusel Cake

2 cups graham cracker crumbs
3/4 cup nuts, chopped
3/4 cup brown sugar, packed
1 1/4 teaspoons cinnamon
3/4 cup butter or margarine
1 (16.5 oz.) package yellow cake mix
5 tablespoons + 1 teaspoon flour
1 cup water
1/4 cup vegetable oil
3 eggs

Preheat oven to 350 degrees F. Generously grease a 13x9x2-inch baking dish. In a medium bowl, combine graham cracker crumbs, nuts, sugar, cinnamon, butter. Set aside.

In a large bowl, blend cake mix, flour, water, oil, and eggs, on low speed until moistened. Continue beating 3 minutes. Pour 1/2 of batter into baking dish. Sprinkle with 1/2 of the crumb mixture. Spread remaining batter evenly over crumbs. Sprinkle remaining crumb mixture over this. Bake at 350 degrees F for 45 to 50 minutes. Cool.

Drizzle cake with the following glaze:

1 cup confectioners' sugar
1 to 2 tablespoons water

Blueberry Streusel

5 tablespoons margarine
1 package yellow or white cake mix
1 (1/4 oz.) package dry yeast
1 1/3 cups flour
2 eggs
2/3 cup very warm water
1 (21 oz.) can blueberry pie filling

Preheat oven to 350 degrees F. Melt margarine in a saucepan and set aside.

Meanwhile, mix together 1 1/2 cups cake mix, yeast, flour, eggs and warm water. Blend at medium speed for 2 minutes. Spread in a 13x9x2-inch baking pan. Cover with blueberry pie filling. Add remaining cake mix to melted margarine and mix to crumbs. Sprinkle over pie mix. Bake for 40 minutes at 350 degrees F.

If desired, while streusel is still warm, drizzle with mixture of 1 cup confectioners' sugar, 1 tablespoon corn syrup and 1 tablespoon water.

Coconut Coffee Cake

1 (16.5 oz.) package white cake mix
5 tablespoons + 1 teaspoon flour
1 (3.4 oz.) box instant coconut cream pudding mix
1 cup water
1/2 cup vegetable oil or canola oil
1 teaspoon vanilla
1 egg

Preheat oven to 350 degrees F. Combine all ingredients and mix together for 8 minutes. Scrape edge of bowl often. Put half of batter in a 13x9x2" baking dish. Sprinkle with half of the following:

1/2 cup sugar
1/2 cup pecans, chopped
1/2 teaspoon cinnamon

Top with rest of batter and rest of topping. Bake 30 minutes at 350 degrees F. Mix together and drizzle with:

1 cup confectioners' sugar
1/2 teaspoon vanilla
2 tablespoons milk

Made in the USA
Las Vegas, NV
20 January 2023